# A BRIEF HISTORY OF PIANO MUSIC

## ESSENTIAL MUSIC HISTORY FOR PIANISTS: BAROQUE THROUGH PRESENT DAY

### Jennifer Boster, NCTM

The Playful Piano
PO Box 12931
Ogden, UT 84412-2931
USA

**Cover image:**
Dame ved Klaver (Anna Syberg) by Fritz Syberg, 1894. Public Domain.
Wikimedia Commons

# Table of Contents

Historically, the Baroque era was a time of powerful European monarchs who supported the arts, and it saw the birth of the scientific method. The paintings, architecture and music of this period were characterized by grandiose design, elaborate decorations, and theatricalism. It was a period of magnificence, extravagance, tragic drama, and objective expressiveness.

The word baroque comes from the Portuguese "barroco," which means "an irregular pearl," or something that is distorted or grotesque. It became the name of this era because of the highly ornamental style of the art and music of the time.

Baroque music had a new clarity of tonality, with bright major and dark minor keys replacing the modal writing of earlier periods.

Some other musical characteristics of the Baroque period include robust rhythm and lots of ornamentation, as well as melodic devices such as repetition, imitation and sequence. Each piece conveys one predominant emotion, and the period's music was as diverse as its society. The first operas were written during this time. Baroque music began the modern musical age.

# BAROQUE ERA   1600 TO 1750

The Baroque era was known as "the golden age of the organ." Bach is one composer who wrote a lot of music for the organ - in fact, he is one of the greatest organ composers who has ever lived. Each pipe of the organ plays a single pitch, and is controlled by the keyboard and pedals. The organ is often called the "king of instruments" because of its size, complexity and power.

The other main keyboard instruments of the time were the harpsichord and the clavichord. Most Baroque keyboard instruments could not achieve dynamic variation with the fingers. The clavichord is the only one that could play some different dynamics, although it is nowhere near the dynamic capability of the later pianoforte and today's pianos. A clavichord's strings are struck, similar to the piano, and the harpsichord's strings are plucked.

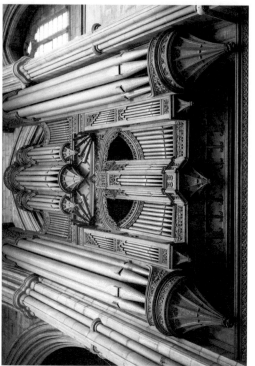

## Playing Baroque Keyboard Music:

Baroque keyboard music has a predominantly polyphonic texture, which means that it is made up of more than one independent line. A great example of this is the Bach Inventions. Because of this polyphony, neither hand is accompanying the other and each hand or musical line is important. A pianist should hear and understand each individual line and practice articulating and bringing each of the lines out at appropriate times.

Much Baroque music does not have originally notated dynamics and articulation because of the instruments of the time. This allows for more individual interpretation of Baroque pieces.

# BAROQUE ERA

## 1600 TO 1750

The dance suite was a popular type of music during this time. It is a collection of Baroque dances of varying character, such as the sarabande, courante, gigue, and allemande. Dance movements in a suite are usually in the same key. Fugues, variations, and freer types of music such as preludes and programmed pieces were also popular, along with figured bass accompaniments.

The main keyboard composers of this period were Johann Sebastian Bach and George Frideric Handel, both born in Germany. Other important keyboard composers include Domenico Scarlatti from Italy (whose music spanned the late Baroque and early Classical eras), François Couperin and Élisabeth Jacquet de La Guerre from France, and Elisabetta de Gambarini from England.

**Elisabeth Jacquet de La Guerre**
1665-1729

**Domenico Scarlatti**
1685-1757

**François Couperin**
1668-1733

**George Frideric Handel**
1685-1759

**Johann Sebastian Bach**
1685-1750

**Elisabetta de Gambarini**
1731-1765

# CLASSICAL ERA 1750 TO 1825

The Classical era happened during the time of the Age of Enlightenment, where many new ideas such as a quest for human happiness, liberty and freedom challenged the monarchs. Historical events that happened during this time include the French Revolution, the American Revolution, and the Industrial Revolution. New technologies, among many other things, advanced music publishing and made pianos more affordable for middle-class families. The pianoforte, with its wide range of expression and dynamics, was developed and started to be used in the late Classical period. Music venues shifted from the royal court to homes and stages of the common man. Music was for everyone, and so the style changed.

One of the earliest pianofortes made by Cristofori

The Classical era was a golden age that produced works of enduring value. The name "classical" refers to ancient Greece and Rome and the values of balance, proportion, and clarity. Important during the Classical period was the value of the common man and the power of human reasoning. The architecture of the time avoided excessive ornamentation and decoration - a big change from Baroque architecture! The classical style is characterized by grace, elegance, simplicity, dignity, symmetry, order, structure and refinement, and the idea that art must imitate nature in some way.

Classical music is distinguished by simple yet prominent folk-like melodies accompanied by broken chords or patterns such as the Alberti bass. Important musical forms of the time include sonata allegro form, rondos, variations, and fantasies. Concertos, string quartets and symphonies were also popular.

## Playing Classical Piano Music:

As opposed to the more complex polyphony of the Baroque period, the music of the Classical period consists of simple homophonic textures. This means that there will usually be one prominent musical line, or melody, in the right hand, accompanied by chords or other patterns in the left hand. Bring out these melodies with control and grace, for the Classical period valued reasoning over emotion. Structure was also super important, so look for the patterns and forms of each piece.

The most important piano composers of the Classical era include Franz Joseph Haydn, Wolfgang Amadeus Mozart, and Ludwig van Beethoven. Beethoven spanned the late Classical and the early Romantic periods. Also of note are Domenico Scarlatti, Muzio Clementi, Carl Philipp Emmanuel Bach, and Hélène de Montgeroult (who taught that the piano can sing).

**Classical-Era Revolution and Musical Change**

The Classical Era was a big time of change; it was a time of many revolutions and the search for individual liberty and human happiness. It was the period in which the pianoforte was developed, changing the possibilities for keyboard music and expression for future pianists and composers.

One remarkable composer, Hélène de Montgeroult, lived through the French Revolution and the Reign of Terror. An incredible keyboard virtuoso, impressive improviser, and esteemed keyboard pedagogue, she played a major role in the development of piano technique and expression at the new instrument: as the new pianofortes were developed, she devoted her teaching and writings to teaching the world that the piano could sing and imitate the expressive Italian singers. Her work helped pave the way for the expressive and emotional music of the Romantic era and for beautiful piano playing throughout the generations.

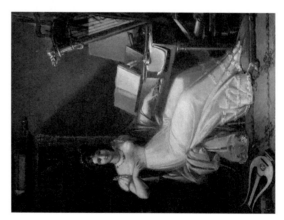

14

**Carl Philipp Emanuel Bach**
1714-1788

**Wolfgang Amadeus Mozart**
1756-1791

**Franz Joseph Haydn**
1732-1809

**Hélène de Montgeroult**
1764-1836

**Muzio Clementi**
1752-1832

**Ludwig van Beethoven**
1770-1827

# ROMANTIC ERA 1800 TO 1925

The Romantic era saw unprecedented changes in the world in technology, travel, science, medicine, and information exchange, and in inventions that changed daily life. With the invention of the phonograph, sound could be recorded, preserved, and reproduced for the first time in history. The sale of printed music became an important source of income for composers. During this time the piano was enlarged, and the pedals perfected.

The name "romantic" comes from the literary "romance," which is a form that tells a long story in verse or prose, and includes legends, folk songs, and fairy tales. The Romantic artistic movement valued imagination and personal expression. It was an era of contrast and contradictions; the logic of the Classical period was disappearing and in its place was expressiveness, virtuosic playing, and a romantic spirit of imagination, drama, and sentiment.

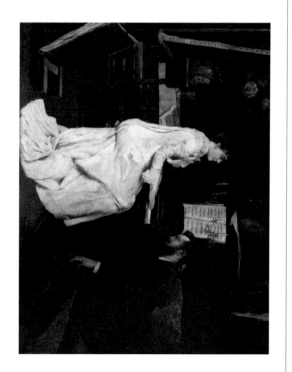

Romantic music is characterized by increased chromatic harmony and complex rhythms, wide variations in dynamics from bombastic to poetic delicacy, and greater originality. Nationalism and program music abound, and new free forms were created such as the rhapsody, fantasy, arabesque, nocturne, and ballade. Also common in the piano literature of the time are etudes, mazurkas, and polonaises. Expansive symphonies, dramatic operas, and passionate songs are common in the non-piano music of the period. This era also saw the growth of public concerts and the view of virtuosic pianists and composers as demigods.

17

# ROMANTIC ERA 1800 TO 1925

There are so many important composers of piano works from the Romantic period! These include Austrian composer Franz Schubert, Polish composer Frederic Chopin, German composers Robert Schumann, Felix Mendelssohn, Johannes Brahms, Fanny Mendelssohn Hensel and Clara Schumann (as well as Beethoven, who spanned both the Classical and Romantic periods), Hungarian composer Franz Liszt, Norwegian composers Edvard Grieg and Agathe Backer-Gröndahl, Russian composers Pyotr Ilyich Tchaikovsky and Sergei Rachmaninoff, French composers Mélanie Bonis and Louise Farrenc, and Venezuelan composer Teresa Carreño. There are, of course, many more, but each of these listed here made significant contributions to piano literature.

**Felix Mendelssohn**
1809-1847

**Franz Schubert**
1797-1828

**Frédéric Chopin**
1810-1849

**Louise Farrenc**
1804-1875

**Robert Schumann**
1810-1856

**Fanny Mendelssohn
Hensel**
1805-1847

# ROMANTIC COMPOSERS

**Johannes Brahms**
1833-1897

**Agathe Backer Grøndahl**
1847-1907

**Clara Wieck Schumann**
1819-1896

**Edvard Grieg**
1843-1907

**Franz Liszt**
1811-1886

**Pyotr Ilyich Tchaikovsky**
1840-1893

**Teresa Carreño**
1853-1917

**Mélanie Bonis**
1858-1937

**Sergei Rachmaninoff**
1873-1943

# ROMANTIC COMPOSERS

# IMPRESSIONISM 1890 TO 1945

Impressionism was not its own era or time period, but instead was a musical and artistic movement during the early Modern era. Influenced by impressionist painters such as Monet, Manet, Renoir, and Degas who used lots of short brush strokes accumulated together to create an impression of something, musical impressionism similarly creates musical impressions of subjects using new approaches and musical techniques.

Some of musical techniques that are characteristic of Impressionism include vague and exotic harmonies. Instead of traditional major and minor scales, impressionist music is often composed using church modes, pentatonic scales or whole tone scales. Rhythms, forms and harmonies are often blurred, and parallel motion is used quite a bit instead of traditional voice leading practices of earlier music. Perhaps above all, there is a greater use of musical color than any previous style.

# IMPRESSIONISM 1890 TO 1945

These musical techniques convey impressions, and create a lot of mood and atmosphere in the music. The music is often delicate and refined. Pieces also commonly have evocative titles, such as Mists, Moonlight, Reflections on the Water, and A Boat on the Ocean.

The composer who is considered the founder of musical impressionism is Claude Debussy of France. Interestingly, he did not like the term impressionism. He said, "There is no theory. You merely need to listen. Pleasure is the law." Other French composers also composed piano music in an impressionist style, including Maurice Ravel, Erik Satie, Germaine Tailleferre and Lili Boulanger. Another important impressionist composer was Charles Tomlinson Griffes of America.

**Claude Debussy**
1862-1918

**Erik Satie**
1866-1925

**Maurice Ravel**
1875-1937

**Charles Tomlinson
Griffes**
1884-1920

**Germaine Tailleferre**
1892-1983

**Lili Boulanger**
1893-1918

# MODERN ERA  20TH CENTURY

The Modern era began in the last decade of the 1800s and continued through the majority of the twentieth century. Musical styles throughout this time period have varied wildly and there is a greater variety of music than in any other musical period. Historically, the twentieth century has been characterized by turmoil and violence (including two world wars), as well as rising democracy. During this time, life became both more efficient and comfortable, and more complex and stressful. There were unprecedented developments in science and technology, including inventions such as computers, motorized transportation, broadcasting, and improved sound recording. People have been able to experience music more than in any previous era; in fact, in the later years of the century especially, music has become so easy to access that there is virtually always music in the background.

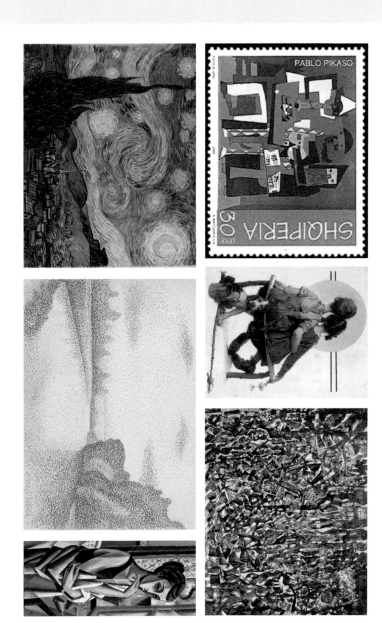

The art and music of the modernist movement can be characterized as fragmented and very diverse. Modernism is not a style, but an attitude. It's all about creating something new, and a quest for novelty. Conventional forms and tonality are often abandoned in this period. Complexity of rhythm, harmony and line have been pushed to new limits. Just as the visual art of this era is very diverse with artists such as Pablo Picasso, Norman Rockwell, Andy Warhol and others, the music can be characterized in many different styles.

# MODERN ERA — 20TH CENTURY

Musical styles common in the Modern era include the following:

- Impressionism
- Expressionism
- Serialism
- Neoclassicism
- Minimalism
- Postmodernism
- Jazz
- Ragtime
- Electronic music

Basically, any type of music that is new or experimental in producing new sounds in new ways is common in this era.

Composers in the Modern era are many and varied. Important composers of piano works during this period include Austrian-born Arnold Schoenberg, Paul Hindemith from Germany, Béla Bartók from Hungary, Russian composers Alexander Scriabin, Sergei Prokofiev and Dmitry Kabalevsky, Armenian composer Aram Khachaturian, Croatian composer Dora Pejačević, and American composers Aaron Copland, Charles Ives, Amy Beach, Scott Joplin, Florence Price and Ruth Crawford Seeger.

**Amy Beach**
1867-1944

**Scott Joplin**
1868-1917

**Alexander Scriabin**
1872-1915

**Arnold Schoenberg**
1874-1951

**Charles Ives**
1874-1954

**Béla Bartók**
1881-1945

# MODERN-ERA COMPOSERS

**Paul Hindemith**
1895-1963

**Sergei Prokofiev**
1891-1953

**Florence Price**
1887-1953

**Dora Pejačević**
1885-1923

**Dmitri Kabalevsky**
1904-1987

**Aram Khachaturian**
1903-1978

**Ruth Crawford Seeger**
1901-1953

**Aaron Copland**
1900-1990

30

# EARLY 21ST CENTURY

Classical music is alive and well, with many living composers currently working and writing important works. Many important twentieth-century composers continue to compose into the twenty-first century, and there are many young composers as well. It is exciting to hear new music today and will be exciting to see what music will continue to be composed in the future.

This list of living composers is a great place to start getting to know what new classical music is being composed today. Of course this list is by no means exhaustive! I encourage you to listen to, learn about, and perform new music.

**Arvo Pärt**
Born 1935

**Philip Glass**
Born 1937

**William Bolcom**
Born 1938

**Judith Lang Zaimont**
Born 1945

**John Adams**
Born 1947

**Alexina Louie**
Born 1949

**Lowell Liebermann**
Born 1961

**Unsuk Chin**
Born 1961

**Max Richter**
Born 1966

**Gabriela Lena Frank**
Born 1972

**Sarah Kirkland Snider**
Born 1973

**Lera Auerbach**
Born 1973

**Missy Mazzoli**
Born 1980

**Caroline Shaw**
Born 1982

**Gabriella Smith**
Born 1991

**Alma Deutscher**
Born 2005

# RECOMMENDED LISTENING

Included on this list is a recommended piano piece to listen to by each composer highlighted in this book. You may access the playlist on YouTube or Apple Music by scanning the QR codes:

Scan to access playlist on Apple Music:

Scan to access playlist on YouTube:

## Baroque Era

**Elisabeth Jacquet de La Guerre**: Pièces de clavecin, Livre 2: Gigue No. 2

**François Couperin**: Pièces de clavecin, Book 3: Le tic toc choc, ou Les maillotins

**Johann Sebastian Bach**: Italian Concerto BWV 971: I. Allegro

**Domenico Scarlatti**: Keyboard Sonata in C Major, K. 159

**George Frideric Handel**: Suite for Harpsichord No. 5 in E Major, HWV 430: IV. Air (with 5 Variations; "Harmonious Blacksmith")

**Elisabetta de Gambarini**: Sonata in C Major, Op. 1 No. 5: III. Spiritoso assai

## Classical Era

**Carl Philipp Emanuel Bach**: Solfeggietto in C Minor

**Franz Joseph Haydn**: Piano Sonata in C, Hob. XVI:50: III. Allegro Molto

**Muzio Clementi**: Sonatina in C Major, Op. 36, No. 1: I. Allegro

**Wolfgang Amadeus Mozart:** Piano Sonata No. 11 in A Major: K. 331: III. Rondo "Alla turca", Allegretto

**Hélène de Montgeroult**: Piano Étude No. 111 in G Minor

**Ludwig van Beethoven**: Sonata No. 14 in C-Sharp Minor, Op. 27 No. 2 "Moonlight": III. Presto

## Romantic Era

**Franz Schubert**: 4 Impromptus, Op. 90, D.899: No. 4 in A-Flat: Allegretto

**Louise Farrenc**: Études Op. 26, No. 17 en Mi Bémol Mineur

**Fanny Mendelssohn Hensel**: The Year (Das Jahr): September (At the River)

**Felix Mendelssohn**: Songs Without Words, Op. 30: No. 6 in F-Sharp Minor (Allegretto tranquil) "Venetian Boat Song"

**Frédéric Chopin**: Ballade No. 3 in A-Flat, Op. 47

**Robert Schumann**: Kinderszenen, Op. 15:7. Träumerei

**Franz Liszt**: 3 Études de concert, S. 144: No 3, Un sospiro (Allegro affettuoso)

**Clara Schumann**: Scherzo No. 2 in C Minor, Op. 14

**Johannes Brahms**: 6 Klavierstücke, Op. 118: No. 2, Intermezzo

**Pyotr Ilyich Tchaikovsky**: Piano Concerto No. 1 in B-Flat Minor, Op. 23: 1. Allegro Non Troppo E Molto Maestoso - Allegro Con Spirito

**Edvard Grieg**: Lyric Pieces Book VIII, Op.65: No. 6, Wedding Day at Troldhaugen

**Agathe Backer Grøndahl**: 3 Morceaux, Op. 15: No. 1, Sérénade

**Teresa Carreño**: Little Waltz (Mi Teresita)

**Mélanie Bonis**: Barcarolle en mi bémol majeur, Op. 71 (A mademoiselle Gabrielle Monchablon)

**Sergei Rachmaninoff**: Prelude in C-Sharp Minor, Op. 3, No. 2

## Impressionism

**Claude Debussy**: Arabesque No. 1

**Erik Satie**: Gymnopédie No. 1

**Maurice Ravel**: Le Tombeau de Couperin, M. 68: I. Prélude

**Charles Tomlinson Griffes**: Roman Sketches, Op. 7, No. 4 Clouds

**Germaine Tailleferre**: Impromptu

**Lili Boulanger**: Trois morceaux pour piano: D'un Jardin Clair

# RECOMMENDED LISTENING

## Modern Era

**Amy Beach**: Hermit Thrush at Eve, Op. 92 No. 1

**Scott Joplin**: Bethena Waltz

**Alexander Scriabin**: Six Preludes, Op. 13: No. 2. Allegro

**Arnold Schoenberg**: Three Piano Pieces, Op. 11: I. Mässige Viertel

**Charles Ives**: Piano Sonata No. 2, "Concord. Mass., 1840-60": Third Movement, "The Alcotts"

**Béla Bartók**: Mikrokosmos, Book 5, BB 105: No. 122. Chords Together and In Opposition

**Dora Pejačević**: 2 Nocturnes, Op. 50: No. 2, Leicht bewegt und verträumt

**Florence Price**: Sonata in E Minor: Andante

**Sergei Prokofiev**: Sonata No. 7, Op. 83: Precipitato

**Paul Hindemith**: Sonata No. 1 for Piano: I. Ruhig bewegte Viertel

**Aaron Copland**: The Cat and the Mouse

**Ruth Crawford Seeger**: Piano Study In Mixed Accents

**Aram Khachaturian**: Toccata

**Dmitri Kabalevsky**: Seven Good-Humoured Variations on a Ukrainian Folksong, Op. 51: No. 4

## 21st Century: Living Composers

**Arvo Pärt**: Für Alina

**Philip Glass**: Etude No. 6

**William Bolcom**: 3 Ghost Rags: No. 1, The Graceful Ghost Rag

**Judith Lang Zaimont**: Sonata for Piano Solo: I. Ricerca

**John Adams**: China Gates

**Alexina Louie**: Star Light, Star Bright: VIII. Blue Sky II

**Lowell Liebermann**: Gargoyles, Op. 29: III. Allegro moderato

**Unsuk Chin**: Piano Etudes: No. 5, Toccata

**Max Richter**: Written On The Sky

**Gabriela Lena Frank**: Sonata Andina: I. Allegro Aymara
**Sarah Kirkland Snider**: The Currents
**Lera Auerbach**: 24 Preludes for Piano, Op. 41: No. 23, Allegretto
**Missy Mazzoli**: A Map of Laughter
**Caroline Shaw**: Gustave Le Gray
**Gabriella Smith**: Imaginary Pancake
**Alma Deutscher**: Sixty Minutes Polka

# IMAGES

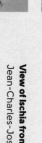

44

**Amy Beach**
29
George Grantham Bain Collection (Library of Congress), Public domain, via Wikimedia Commons

**Scott Joplin, 7 June 1903**
29
Unknown authorUnknown author, Public domain, via Wikimedia Commons

**Alexander Scriabin**
29
Public domain, via Wikimedia Commons

**Arnold Schoenberg, 1948**
29
Florence Homolka, Attribution, via Wikimedia Commons

**Charles Edward Ives, National Portrait Gallery**
29
Clara Sipprell, CC0, via Wikimedia Commons

**Béla Bartók**
29
Unknown authorUnknown author, Public domain, via Wikimedia Commons

**Dora Pejačević**
30
Miguel Biarnés, CC BY-SA 4.0 <https://creativecommons.org/licenses/by-sa/4.0>, via Wikimedia Commons

**Sergei Prokofiev circa 1918 over chair**
30
Bain News Service, publisher, Public domain, via Wikimedia Commons

**Paul Hindemith USA**
30
See page for author, CC BY-SA 3.0 <http://creativecommons.org/licenses/by-sa/3.0/>, via Wikimedia Commons

**Aaron Copland in 1962**
30
CBS Television, Public domain, via Wikimedia Commons

Jenny Boster has been playing the piano and creating things ever since she was a little girl. She loves combining her interests to create fun and original resources for piano teachers. She has loved teaching piano lessons for twenty-five years. Jenny has a Bachelor of Music degree in Piano Performance from Brigham Young University and is a Nationally-Certified Teacher of Music. She frequently speaks at music teacher conferences and has become an advocate of female composers. Jenny is passionate about encouraging students to listen to and gain a love for classical music. Her greatest joys are her husband, Jonathan, and being a mother to her five children.

Find Jenny online at theplayfulpiano.com and on Instagram @theplayfulpiano.

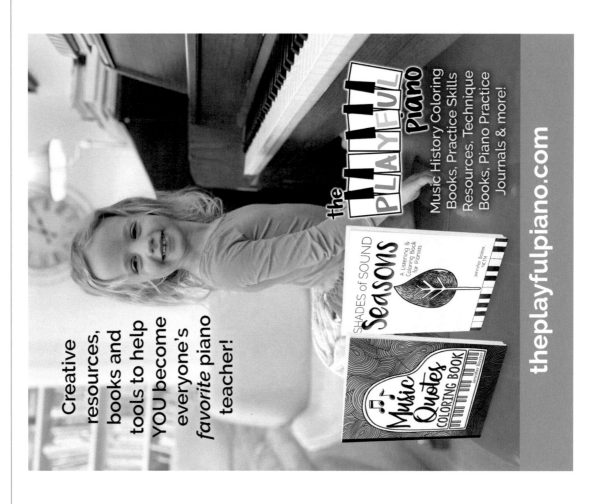

Made in United States
Cleveland, OH
27 November 2024

1098714 3R00031